THE FAQ GUIDE

(for small businesses)

Dinma Nmaele-Afam

DNA Imprints (publisher)

THE FAQ GUIDE

COPYRIGHT 2022

No part of this document should be reproduced, printed or distributed without the author's permission.

DNA Imprints would like to hear from you:

@Dinma Nmaele-Afam on Linkedin

Email: dnaimprints@gmail.com

TABLE OF CONTENT

Dedication

Acknowledgement

Introduction

Chapter 1: History of FAQ.

Chapter 2: Who needs an FAQ?

Chapter 3: Why should you have an FAQ page?

Chapter 4: FAQ, the customer care your business needs.

Chapter 5: Styles of writing FAQ.

Chapter 6: Step by step guide on how to write your FAQ.

Chapter 7: Catchy Headings.

Chapter 8: 25 Examples to help guide you.

Chapter 9: Real FAQ examples.

Chapter 10: FAQ without a website.

Conclusion

Glossary

An uncertain customer is a prospect for your competition_DNA Imprints

To keep customers to yourself, you need a structure that works even in your absence.

A system that works round the clock.

A crucial part of that system is an FAQ!

Get an FAQ for your business today.

DEDICATION

To small business owners, trying to put structure to their business.

It will pay someday.

ACKNOWLEDGEMENT

The Don, Emeka Nobis, if you doubt the magnitude of the influence you wield, through your Facebook posts on book writing and shameless marketing. Here I am!

Harirat Ogunlade, for being the shove I needed to finish this book. Thank you.

INTRODUCTION

For any business to thrive,its customers need to be satisfied.

For that to happen,your business must ensure that the transaction is seamless and memorable for the customer.

In order to achieve this,you need to build a working system.One that is built to last.

One component of a working system in a business is a well written & positioned FAQ,on your website,or Facebook page, or in your physical space.

- Your business will thank you for it !
- Your brand will grow because of it!
- Your customers will appreciate you for caring enough about them that you have proactively offered answers to any question they may have.

Open your mind to the possibilities an FAQ can

do for your business.

CHAPTER 1: HISTORY OF FAQ

Frequently Asked Questions commonly known as FAQ {pronounced F-A-Q or fack} is a list of predicted questions and answers found in website pages, email lists, online forums, events, businesses, books. Most recently is the addition of the FAQ option on social media platforms such as Facebook. This option is only found on professional pages.

This was not always the case, the compilation of Q&A, which is primarily what FAQ is about, dates back to 1648;the discovery of witches by Matthew Hopkins was written as a list of Q&A. Many old catechism books (books used to teach children or newly converted adults, the doctrine of the Church) still in existence today in the Catholic Church were written as a list of Q&A.

Plato's dialogues date back even further.

From 1982, due to the cost of storage, NASA developed the FAQ to avoid repeating answers to new users on the email on the email list by Eugene Miya; these FAQs were posted monthly, weekly and at some point daily.

Over time the accumulated FAQ across all Usenet newsgroups sparked the creation of the answers moderated newsgroups such as comp.answers, misc.answers, sci.answers for cross posting collecting FAQ across respective comp.misc & sci.newsgroups.

Today, more and more people have gone with the flow & tweaked it to suit their personal / professional needs.

An FAQ has become an important component of websites, either as a standalone page or as a website section with multiple subpages per question or topic.

CHAPTER 2: WHO NEEDS AN FAQ?

Previously FAQ was a tool used only by big brands without adequate customer care agents or sales personnel to attend to the numerous questions that customers had.

These brands understood the golden rule of business "a customer is the bloodline of any business" so every business has to satisfy its customers.

One way of doing this effectively was by giving out all the information about a product or service.

Every customer wants to make an informed purchase. No customer wants to waste their money on a product/service they would not use or go through the trouble of purchasing a product/service and seeking a refund later.

No business also wants a bad review, angry

customers and low recommendations.

So the best way to cover both ends was to put in place a list of questions & answers; therefore helping the business save
precious time that would have been used to answer numerous enquiry calls/emails and channel it to other things.

- Access to this list means that a customer will make an informed purchase.

These days of entrepreneurships, start-ups, ever budding small business, technologies and search results gotten at the click of a button. No one should stay behind.

Most small businesses are owned and operated solely by one, two or a few persons who cannot run a business and efficiently attend to all the enquiry calls of their customers. These big brands are still struggling to meet up with the influx of customer's enquiries and complaints on a daily basis, no matter how many agents they have on ground. How then is a small business supposed to meet up?

The answer is FAQ!

Your business needs a FAQ.

Your event needs a FAQ.

Your book needs FAQ.

Your class needs an FAQ

Every money-making venture needs an FAQ.

CHAPTER 3: WHY YOU NEED AN FAQ.

Time is precious! is money and opportunity waits for no one.

Do not waste valuable time attending to customers' enquiries instead of on selling your products and services.

Humans are fallible, that includes you and your staff, no one can answer the phone or check emails/messages 24 hours daily especially for sole proprietorship businesses.

Your customers, (prospects and loyal customers alike) want to know more about your business.

Every customer should buy from you on full disclosure.

Can your business boast of that?

For every business is cut out to make profit.

You must think about the FAQ. It is a need that must be fulfilled.

When you think big for your business, you think FAQ.

When you think about structure. Think FAQ.

When you think of continuity, think FAQ.

When you think SEO, think FAQ.

When you think of doing business with ease, think FAQ.

When you think customer satisfaction, think FAQ.

When you think transparency in business, think FAQ'

This is only a few highlighted reasons for an FAQ.

1. Structure

Any business built to last must consider having a well written FAQ.

Humans are drawn to a business with a good structure; no customer wants to buy from a business that appears disorganized.

Let's take a look at these scenarios

Hello, ma. I want to purchase 5 cartons of smoked

fish from you. I do not need up to 4 cartons but I decided to go above three cartons because I want a larger discount for buying more than three cartons which is the lowest number of cartons available for sale"

Then your salesperson says "oh, sorry ma, three is the least we sell at a discounted price. And you want to add two for a larger discount, let me get back to you on that.

Scenario 2; your page/website has an FAQ.

No 2 question is; how many cartons of fish do I buy from fish affairs at a discounted rate.

Answer;

At fish affairs, we sell 12, half a dozen or minimum of 3 cartons.

Our discount goes only to sales of a dozen or half a dozen. If you decide to add an extra to any of these, you will only get a discount on o you at the offer made while the extras will be given to you at retail price. For more tips on how to enjoy extra discount, check **Q.10**

I can't afford to buy 6 cartons of fish monthly, but I am a loyal customer. How else can I enjoy this discount?

Answer

At fish affairs, we take pride in our customer satisfaction, to best serve our loyal customers so we have come up with several ways for such customers to enjoy a discount

> 1. We have a sharing formula {we will sell at a discounted rate and share the 12 cartons to several fish vendors but to enjoy this, each vendor is expected to pay for the number of cartons they need on or before 1st of every month.
> 2. Every Thursday from 12 noon, we sell at giveaway prices; you can come to our store at…or pay online to enjoy this discount. Promo sales ends at 5pm'

Who do you think is likely to make more sales?

The sales agent might not be able to reach that customer back immediately and has a high chance of losing her.

While business no 2. need not worry about a customer calling to even make enquiry because what the customer needs to know is already out there.

So before that customer calls to place an order, she has gone through the FAQ and has made her decision on what quantity she can afford.,

If she wants a discount how and when she can get it.

This also has an advantage for a business owner, you look organized to your customers. You look experienced.

You look like you have been in the business for a while and know your onions.

Having your FAQ handy means you have the right answers at your fingertips, you never have to put your customers on hold or have to call them back.

A potential person can change their mind in a minute. Don't let your money as a business owner slip away.

Who wouldn't want to do business with such a person?

That is the beauty of an FAQ.

Another way an FAQ puts structure in your business is that it forces you to make difficult decisions on important matters before it happens. Decisions such as:

- Pricing i.e. placing a flat price on your Products and services.
- Return Policies
- Open days and time.
- Information on varieties and up sells.
- Better customer service.
- Hotline
- Delivery options.
- Global or local coverage
- Payment options
- Emergency contact channel i.e. self help,hotline.
- Information to share and not share.

- Prevent Discrepancies

2. Saves time

An FAQ saves you a lot of time; you do not have to spend so much time on enquiry calls. You will instead channel that time in attending to the needs of customers and making money.

There is no brand without an FAQ.

For example; Gotv, one of the biggest media companies in Africa with hundreds of customer care agents, walk-in locations, representatives, affiliated businesses, physical help centers, self help methods, a dedicated channel for self help on their services and adverts on promos and new offers.

It isn't enough; their website still carries an FAQ. With all these resources at hand, they have taken care of the common enquiries their customers would have.

Customer care agents now have more time on their hands to promptly handle more important issues, technical problems and closing deals which would in turn fetch GOTV more money.

Plus over time, they will cut down on the number of agents they will have to pay monthly because these other resources are efficient, available, and easier to access.

THE FAQ GUIDE

This is a big business and they have all these resources on their hands. Yet they want to serve their customers, they do not want a stranded customer, they do not want a sad customer.

Take for instance, a user of MTN service, one of Africa's giant telecommunication companies in the middle of a jam and wants to know how to switch to their postpaid service.

He has two options: call the customer care number and wait for his turn (this could take up to 40 mins-1 hour)

2. go through their FAQ,from where he is being led to a self-help cie on how to do it himself.(answer can be gotten at the click of a button).

In the case of an emergency,which would he turn to?

If you were that MTN customer,who route would you take?

You will choose the latter,it's faster and saves you a lot of time..

On the other end the customer care agent has more time to attend to more pressing calls,texts and emails promptly.

In your small business,a pap business.

You have one of two sales persons in your store,they manage it, inventory,sales, customer service etc.

They barely have time for breaks, would you rather they spend hours on the phone or on emails attending to enquiries on the varieties, sizes and prices of pap?

Instead of handling orders & deliveries and making actual sales.

In the case of a sole proprietorship kind of business, where you are the manufacturer, sales person, delivery guy, teller, receptionist etc.

Would you have the time and mental energy to always answer enquiries?

Even on a bad day with no sales, consider the mental drain 9f talking to 5 customers a day, repeating the same thing over and over and over again.

You could do that for a cumulative period of several hours a day & end up without a sale from those prospects..

That is just one day!

Imagine doing it for several months.

Also as human, you can't always be available or indisposed to attend to all of your customer's enquiries.

The question now is; As a small business owner what resources do you have?

What resources have you provided to ease business for your customers?

How are you saving time for more important issues?

How many hours do you spend every day on the phone attending to several similar enquiries from different customers?

3. An FAQ brings Perspective

This perspective helps with making difficult choices as a business owner.

You understand you are building a brand so every detail needs to be considered.

From pricing to terms and conditions, to delivery to insurance policy. The list is endless.

Small business owners in Nigeria are faced with a lot of challenges and so they hardly want to go through the trouble of setting a standard for a new business barely bringing in the big bucks.

What we fail to understand is; the best way to prepare for uncertainties is to make provisions for it, to plan for it, so that when we are faced with these challenges, it is easier to handle.

In writing an FAQ, these things are put into consideration, they include

Pricing: every business should have a price list. Develop one, include delivery rates per location & **weight** of order, insurance percentage for logistics, custom/special orders up-sells, promo offers, bonus, installation rates {for those in service based businesses} etc. Have this information ready and available.

Delivery: have a list of where your business can deliver. Start by asking yourself, am I a Local or Global business?

If you are local, that would mean your country, e.g. Nigeria.

Now, in Nigeria, how many states can I deliver my goods to?

If your business is global, how many continents?

What countries?

Drop off & Pick up points.

Logistics partners [in states where you do not have pick-up or drop off points.

How to track a delivery?

How long a delivery to each location would take?

Steps to take, when you have to track your goods.

Payment options

To meet the needs of a wider audience, a business owner must have several payment options.

Business has gone beyond cash or card only!

Transfer option is also now beyond your local currency.

Wire options too are getting limitless so every business owner needs to keep up.

Create several options and keep it handy. You should have at least two local bank accounts, a domiciliary account for foreign currency.

Refund policy:

What are the terms and conditions for a refund?

Discount and Promos:

Who is eligible?

What qualifies a customer?

What quantity does a customer pay before he is eligible for a discount?

How many times does he have to patronize your business to get a discount?

Are there specific days /periods/timeframe for these promos? Etc.

Insurance policy

Is there an existing insurance policy you operate?

Where does the customer come in?

Is it included in the price of goods?

How many percent is a customer to pay on insurance?

Is there third party insurance?

4. Prevents bad review:

One bad thing can ruin years of hard work,good service and great customer relationships in a business.

Your business empire,which took you years to build, can crash in a day.

In business,not every publicity is good publicity.

I have written a number of damage control and apologies for my clients to their customers and I have come to realize a great number of those would have been avoided if there was better communication.

Some customers,even with a manual in their hands, would still ask a lot of questions and you should answer them.

Break it down into tiny bits to prevent misunderstanding.

Let your FAQ answer all of their questions,it's your business so you are probably more of an expert on that product /service.

Be as honest as you can possibly be without spilling the secrets of your business.

Whenever a customer patronizes you,it should be based on full disclosure and proper knowledge so no one comes dragging you into the mud in the future and winning you at it.

5. Earn your customer's trust:

For a digital product or business strictly online,you need to earn your customers trust and one surefire way of doing that is to put out all the information that customer needs to know on your product/service.

Put it all in your FAQ.

They see for themselves that you have nothing to hide.

They do business with you,with both eyes open.

From what we have seen recently online,most of the businesses that succeeded in defrauding people were those whose clients were not privy to the necessary information.

An FAQ sets you apart,by putting out the answers to the questions your customers are asking.

6. Provides new insight:

As you write your FAQ,your mind begins to open up to opportunities in your business.

It is said that we learn everyday.

This is so true because as you put down the questions,you realize there are things that should be added to your business.

Several icings on your cake.

It could be an upsell, a product or service that goes hand in hand with what you are already offering.

Skills you already have and can add to what you do.

This is particularly for businesses that sell products.

For instance: If you sell perfumes only.

In drafting your FAQ, you will realize that you could add diffusers, humidifiers, scent balls etc because those things go hand in hand.

A customer who wants one is mostly likely to ask for the other so you can introduce those alongside the perfumes you sell.

For Services, it's the same. At DNA Imprints, we write official letters, in writing their FAQ, they realize their clients would want them to write emails too.

So, let's do both.

7. Brings Clarity

As you write down the questions of your FAQ, you might be tempted to include more products and services because an FAQ is a means of advertisement and once you put it out there, it may take a while before you update it so you want to put it all out there.

By the time you begin to put in your answers you are

clear on what you can deliver and you start to cut off the distractions.

8. Drives internal page view & visibility.:

In a phrase"the more the merrier"

The more the posts, keywords,Q & A, associated with your business that you have online,the more visibility you enjoy.

The more your business is optimized for visibility on the internet.

9. FAQ optimizes SEO

SEO (Search Engine Optimization).

A lot of people use voice search when searching for answers on the Web.

Now,an FAQ has an advantage because it was basically questions and answers.

So when a customer searches, how do I make chips?

The answer is likely to be an explanatory tutorial contained in the FAQ of a fast food joint on how to make chips.

DINMA NMAELE

CHAPTER 4: FAQ, THE CUSTOMER CARE SERVICE YOUR BUSINESS NEEDS.

We all know several brands, really big brands I must add with impeccable customer care service and agents with sweet voices. Maybe it isn't always so in reality but you get the point.

Those are big brands with loads of cash to employ customer care agents, which is a luxury small businesses cannot afford.

Does that mean there is no hope for small

businesses? If there is. It is called FAQ.

FAQ, is the customer care service every small business can afford!

There is hope with a well written FAQ and well trained employees to point your customers to the right places for answers.

The job of a customer care agent is to attend to the needs of customers, which include answering enquiries, taking complaints, resolving customers issues and helping a customer make informed decisions on your products/services. All of these can be done by your FAQ.

The question is "can your small business afford to employ a customer care agent?

If you can, one customer care agent attends to the needs of your customers.

If by some super power, they can.

How long can you afford to pay this agent?

Would you rather, an FAQ that requires a one time writing with regular updates or a CSA on your monthly payroll..

All of your employees can do the job of a customer care agent if properly trained to optimize the use of your FAQ by referring your customers there, the right way and at the right time.

A well written FAQ on your website or official

business page on Facebook might be the convincing a customer needs to hop on your train.

Hassle free transactions are all every customer and business owner desires.

One way to make that happen is ensuring your FAQ has all the answers your customers need.

An FAQ solves your customers enquiry without a monthly paycheck.

By whatever means your customers find you,your FAQ will sort out their needs.

If they come through your website,they get the answers to make an informed choice on your products and services because your FAQ is in plain sight.

If they got to know about your business through recommendation or referral. When they contact you through phone or email/message or simply walk into your store.

You can provide them with whatever form of FAQ you have.

While you sort out orders, do inventories and make money.

Check **Chapter 5**,for styles of FAQ.

CHAPTER 5: STYLES OF WRITING FAQ.

In writing the FAQ, I would liken it to the Bible quote that says " how far as your eye can see". Your only limit is you.

Here are some:

1. Video FAQ
   1. In FAQ, if your customers can ask it, you should answer it.

If you offer products that require a hands on services like installation, then Video should make up a part of your FAQ.

In whatever form, live or animation, graphics etc. Make one and add it to your FAQ.

In such businesses, all you need to lose customers to competition is the inability to proffer solutions.

It's impossible to do manual installations for all your customers, especially the ones in far locations, so an explanatory video in your FAQ will help.
For instance,you import Tricycles into Abuja,Nigeria.
Tricycles come into the country, disassembled to reduce the cost of shipment and to bring in more.
When they come in,you can choose to assemble some and sell to those close to your location..

Those who are in other states who want to buy directly from you as an importer would have to buy it in its original state in order to reduce the high cost of delivery across states.
An explanatory Do-it-yourself video on your page,"How to assemble a Tricycle at home" will largely increase your customer base as you have addressed a pressing need.
Who wouldn't want to buy from a guy who can teach me to install it myself.
I can even learn a new skill and make money from helping others install theirs once I have successfully done mine.

2. Pictorial FAQ:

We have heard the saying "A picture tells a thousand words"

Pictures are catchy,take little space,consume less data and are straight to the point.

In writing FAQs,you can make use of pictures.

- As a step by step guide showing a customer what they need to know through the use of pictures.

For example:you can use pictures to show the varieties of products/ services you have or offer.

- You can use pictures to illustrate a Do-It - Yourself to teach your customers how to best utilize your products and services.
- In graphics like a price list, opening days,delivery locations etc

2. Catalog

Catalogs are often used to show pictures of products and services.

To spice it up,you can project your FAQ in a catalog style,where your customers can view beautiful, enchanting pictures of your products and services,with a blend of Q &A on your products & services.

The pictures included should be enticing enough to keep your customers from flipping through the pages of your catalog.

For this style,it's important that your pictures are vivid,catchy,easy on the eyes as they scroll through the pages of your printed FAQ or online.

This is suitable for Businesses like beauty care,skin products,interior designing,food & pastries

4. Links

This style of FAQ works great for shortening the length of your questions and answers.

Here is how it works:You only make a few questions and answers visible.
Then input links to several pages for further explanation.
Some answers are lengthy and might require a blog post or article to help break down the problem to a customer.
This is great too for directing customers outside your page. For instance,a question that requires a video to better answer it may not be on your page but can be found on YouTube.
Inserting a link to the video under a question or answer in your FAQ page is a great way of giving your customer the best answer they need.

5. Pamphlet: This works in print form. Fancy Pamphlet at your offline location with catchy headings like"Let's get you started" or "All you need to know".

These Pamphlets should be kept in a strategic position in your store,where it is easily accessible to your clients as soon as they walk in. The front desk,on stools in the reception or waiting arenas,inside your catalogs. In the restroom etc.

{Gotta keep reading}

6. Electronic Display/ TV: Just like adverts. An FAQ can be displayed via electronic billboards, projectors,movable TVs.

These styles work better for small businesses if placed close to your business place.

Especially a business with a conducive waiting area where customers can relax and stare at your FAQ.

Examples of such businesses are Commercial Banks, Plazas, Amusement parks, Relaxation areas like a spa, Restaurants,Schools etc.

You can switch between your FAQ and your advert.

Some are to stick in the minds of your customers.

A list of Q & A: Last but not the least.
The good old compilation of Q&A.
This one is tricky.

It should be written in conversational style.
Like you are attending to the customer in person.
Catchy phrases here or there,light humor, no bogus words.
This isn't the time to show you are Havard Material,make it enjoyable to read,easy to understand.
Paper should be thick,glossy and bright coloured.
If you can pull it off,it is a great and affordable way to do your FAQ in print.

You can combine two or more styles of FAQ for your business.

Like they say "Two heads are better than one".

CHAPTER 6: STEP BY STEP GUIDE ON HOW TO WRITE YOUR FAQ.

1. Determine your Questions

Firstly, you must have in mind that there is no dumb question in the FAQ, if one customer can think of it, they will ask it.

Make a long list of questions; i.e. questions asked by previous customers and prospects.

By friends or family who have tested your products.

Make informed guesses about what your customers would ask you.

Ask your employees.

Ask people who have been in the business longer than you have.{this could be an eye opener on areas where you need development}

If this is a new business yet to hit the ground, you could offer free samples of your products and services and in return ask for honest reviews.

In between those lines, you will find several questions that need to be answered.

Another way of compiling an FAQ is to write down all the information of your business.

Opening days & hours: how many times a week do you open shop?

Location: Physical or online [address}

Contact information: hotline, phone number, social media handle, pager etc.

Products & services:make a list of all you sell or do.

Variants: are they varieties of what you sell or offer.

Upsells: are there things that go hand in hand with what you do or sell.

Promos & Discount: what qualifies customers for discounts and promos.

Pricing: How much does each of your goods and services cost {make a list of all you sell or do, every single thing and their prices}.

LOCATION: the address of your store's physical location. Headquarters, branches etc.

Partners: do you have a franchise?

What similar product/Service do you offer?

Do you observe the same standards?

What are the Similarities and Differences?

What locations are your franchises?

Can I order something from one store and get it from another?

Delivery: do you do delivery?

What kind of delivery?

Global or local?

Door to door delivery or do you use logistics companies?

Is there an extra cost for delivery? etc

Refund policy: what are the terms and conditions for which you will grant a customer a refund?

Payment details: how do you wish to get paid? Cash or Wire transfer or both?Details on any or both.

Categorize your Questions
One way to effectively position your FAQ to satisfy your customer's needs is to neatly place your Q & A in categories.

Your customers should not have to scroll through pages upon pages for questions and answers that are related.

Your Q & A should be positioned in such a way that all related questions and answers are placed closely together alongside each other depending on the interface of your website.

You placed all related Q & A under a single category.

For example: Under the Category {Products} for the FAQ of DNA Imprints Nmaele Media {DNA Imprints},a media outfit that delivers Writing and Speaking services.

Services::
    1. Does DNA Imprints write FAQ?
Yes. DNA Imprints offers a variety of writing services and FAQ is also an integral part of what we do at DNA Imprints.

    2. What other Writing services do you offer at DNA Imprints
- At DNA Imprints,we write:
- Official Letters/ Emails.
- Speeches.
- We do Editing/ Proofreading.
- Speech Presentation
- AudiobookNarration.
- Amazon KDP services.
- DNA Imprints also has published works;The Rushed Education,The FAQ Guide amongst others.

    • **Speech:**
    3. Can DNA Imprints do a speech presentation

of a speech not written by them?
Speech presentation is one of the services we offer at DNA Imprints whether it was written by us or not.

4. How long does it take for DNA Imprints to prepare for a speech?

For a speech written by us, 3-4 days.
This process involves several back and forth to the venue.
Prepping for the crowd.
Understanding the dynamics of the audience etc.

For a speech not written by us, we will prefer a head start of 5 days -1 week. There are exceptions for premium service.

5. Does DNA Imprints serve only the needs of individual bodies only?

No, DNA Imprints serves both individual and corporate bodies.

6. Can DNA Imprints host events?

Yes. Official events only!
Campaigns, Luncheons, Forums,
Conferences, Official Dinners etc.

Contact Information:

1. How can I reach DNA Imprints Media Services?

You can reach DNA Imprints through our hotline:08058135742{WhatsApp or call} 08095369484.{text only).or via any of our social media pages on Facebook, Twitter, LinkedIn &

Tiktok@DNA Imprints Nmaele

2 . Can I book an appointment for a physical meeting?
At DNA Imprints,we understand we offer services of convenience so on the premium plan,we will come to you at a safe location.
You can set an appointment through any of the above channels and we will have a physical meeting in Abuja.

In the above example,there were two categories and a sub category in Speech.
Imagine how frustrating it would be for a customer to go back and forth while scrolling through the DNA Imprints Media FAQ page if the questions from both categories were mixed up,with the Q&A from both categories intertwined.
That's why it's important to categorize the FAQ.

Others forms of category can be placed this:
Shipping and Refund policy.
Pricing
Promotions and Discounts.
Sizing
Products and Services.

Note: scrolling through a long list of related Q&A in a single place before getting to another category is as tiresome as going back and forth through a jumbled FAQ..

To prevent this from happening,here are several

methods to use:
For websites
Let the questions in each category be embedded in that category.
For example: Pricing
Products
Shipping etc.
The customer should find all they need to know on Pricing when they click on Pricing.

1. You can reduce the number of questions in the FAQ page/ section and insert links to several landing pages where your customers can find the rest of the Q&A.
2. You can insert links to blog posts where the answers to the questions your customers need are fully explained.

For a Facebook page,the steps are similar to no 1.
You can make several posts online. In those posts,you can categorize your FAQ.

Each post can contain one or two categories per post and copy the links.
Make one final post on your FAQ containing all the categories and insert the links in the answers so your customer can reach the questions and answers when they click on each category.

2. Highlight or link the most popular questions

The idea of an FAQ page is to put the most frequently asked questions out there,in the customer's face where they can't miss it.

This takes us to the third way.

In writing your FAQ, what are the most frequently asked 5-10 questions?

Highlight them.

Put them first.

Most frequently asked to least frequently asked questions.

The rest? Use inserted links to take the customer to the right information.

Note: scrolling through a long list of related Q&A in a single place before getting to another category is as tiresome as going back and forth through a jumbled FAQ..

To prevent this from happening, here are several methods to use:

    1. For websites

Let the questions in each category be embedded in that category.

    For example: Pricing
        Products
        Shipping etc.

The customer should find all they need to know on Pricing when they click on Pricing.

    2. You can reduce the number of questions in the FAQ page/ section and insert links to several landing pages where your

customers can find the rest of the Q&A.
3. You can insert links to blog posts where the answers to the questions your customers need are fully explained.

For a Facebook page,the steps are similar to no 2.
You can make several posts online. In those posts,you can highlight your most popular questions in your FAQ.

Each post can contain one or two categories per post and copy the links.
Make one final post on your FAQ containing all the categories and insert the links in the answers so your customer can reach the questions and answers when they click on each category.

3 . Add a search bar/product locator:
This How is particularly for websites.
- If your FAQ page /sections contain a lot of questions and are too lengthy.
- You do not want your customers to spend so much time searching for questions and answers
- Some of the Q&A are hidden.

Then include a search or navigation bar to make visiting your website and knowing more about your business stress free.

4. Let your FAQ represent your brand:

For pictorial FAQ; use brand colors.
For price list: Use fliers done in brand colors with prices per

products/services.
This can be done for location and delivery prices.

If you offer Swift services, let your FAQ prove that.
Let your customers get their answers swiftly.

Does your brand offer services of convenience? Let your FAQ make transacting business with you easy.

Is your business about accessibility, let your FAQ help make your business accessible.
The list is endless.

4. Add a Search bar/Product locator:

This 'how' is particularly for FAQ on websites, if your FAQ section (the Q&A) is too lengthy or you simply want to reduce the length of visible Q &A .

Maybe you want to ease the stress of your customers.

You don't want them spending so much time looking for answers..

Then include a search or navigation bar, that will make visiting your page or knowing more about your business stress **free**.

5. Review and improve:

Always do a review of your FAQ. Find out from your customers which Q &A was most helpful to them.

For websites, do a check on the questions with the

most clicks.

That should help you track down the most frequently asked questions and least frequently asked questions.

Then you do a reshuffle of your Q&A from FAQ to LAQ.

6. Update regularly

An out- of - date FAQ page is worse than having not having an FAQ at all.

An outdated FAQ is useless.

Update your FAQ as regularly as you make changes in your business.

If you add a new product / service, update your FAQ.

If there are new improvements, update your FAQ.

Sometimes, an LAQ becomes very popular and is now frequently asked, updating your FAQ by taking that question to the top.

You make changes in your payment details, return policy, shipping etc, update your FAQ.

No matter how small or big the change may be, a customer would like to know. Ensure you add it to your FAQ.

7. Answer your FAQ positively

THE FAQ GUIDE

Without exposing the shortcomings of your business (products / service) ,answer every question honestly but in a positive light.

For instance, a customer having gone through DNA Imprints Media Services still wants to know if he can add extra to the pack he chose.

Here it goes; Q: I chose an FAQ pack but I want an extra 5

Q & A to be added to my FAQ pack.

Is there a way to make it happen?

A: No we can't go beyond the Q & A in each pack because of the following reasons.

- Each question cost N334 and that amount is bit round figure that will amount touch if the questions are not much.

  { Too much information,that your client don't need to know}

- You should get the next pack instead. {comes off as rude}

- At DNA Imprints,we are professionals who treat each work as special pouring so much into it.

  The questions and answers that make up an FAQ are carefully crafted and we need to pay these professionals who do the work handsomely,we can't afford to go through all that for a few extra

49

Q &A and less pay.

{ Too much information,that your client don't need to know you are exposing your secrets }

Instead in your forethinking ,when writing your FAQ.

You already have a package for such clients.

Q: I chose an FAQ pack but I want an extra 5

Q & A to be added to my FAQ pack.

Is there a way to make it happen?

A: At DNA Imprints, our FAQ pack was pre designed by putting a lot of factors into consideration.

- The number of Q &A that would cover the most frequently asked questions of a business in one view.
- The time ,effort and research it takes to finish a pack.
- The value of each pack while putting into consideration what customers would be willing to pay for a certain number OF Q&A. etc.

On a client's behest,we will do a custom pack.Every additional 3 Q&A costs 1000.

CHAPTER 7: CATCHY HEADINGS

The term FAQ is sometimes associated with a long list of Q & A.
In truth, that's what it is.

Lengthy can mean boring so let's do a mental trick.

Instead of the heading 'FAQ' aka the boring list of Q&A, you better go through and figure out what you want.

Here are some catchy headings to make customers click before they blink. Interesting enough to catch a customer's attention and make them believe ,'Oh I need to go through this' or 'Hey,I just might get the answer I need here'

1. How may we help?

2. Everything you need to know.

3. What's new?

4. What can we help you with today?

5. What you should know.

6. Help Topics.

7. Welcome, how can we help you?

8. FAQ: We thought you'd never ask.

9. Get Help.

    10.   Support:Ask us anything.

    11.   Explore.

    12.   Discover.

    13.   Self help/care.

THE FAQ GUIDE

14. Complete guide.

15. Help Center.

16. Don't want to join the customer care agent's queue?

17. Having problems?

18. Need a hand?

19. Interact with us.

20. Let's get you started.

You can even use the ' i' ' sign that represents help. Or go dramatic by using a light bulb?

CHAPTER 8 EXAMPLES TO GUIDE YOU.

The FAQ of these businesses was preselected to help guide you in writing yours.

I have no affiliation with these brands. They were simply used to show you how it's done.

You still have to give your FAQ a personal touch through your style of writing, use of colors and brand representation.

Let's go

Here are 25 brands, you may recognize a few and this is your first time seeing them, you can check them out.

1. Piggyvest
The first thing you notice about Piggy Vest FAQ is how the questions in the search bar pops up and changes by itself.
They really want to make things easy.
- The FAQ is categorized into 16.
- Questions are written in bold font, also keywords in the

THE FAQ GUIDE

answer section are done in bold too.
- When you click on any of the categories. You still get to see a list of the other categories in vertical form reminding you of where else you could go to for answers.

Withdrawals   Piggy Points   Referral Pr

Can I choose any amount to withdraw per time?

Yes, you can!

Simply log into your account and click on the withdraw option, then input the amount you want to withdraw.

PS: The minimum amount that can be accessed from your Piggybank and Flex Naira wallets is N3000 and N2000 respectively.

2. DSTV
The website is very colorful and so when you get to the FAQ section and see Welcome! Let's get you started in blue,(the Brand's color),you truly believe it.
The second question is done, pictorial style as you would see

55

below, followed by a catchy category of help resources you can tap on and really get started titled, "stay engaged with us".

The quote is relatable to the brand because it provides entertainment which in turn engages us.

Next : Our self service platforms.

Let's get you started

What's a Smartcard number?
Your Smartcard number is on the reverse of your smartcard, below the barcode and is linked to your decoder and your customer number that was created with MultiChoice when you initiated your DStv subscription.

When to use your Smartcard number?
When logging into our digital platforms to make a payment, fix decoder errors, change package and more, you will always need to enter your smartcard number, mobile number, or surname.

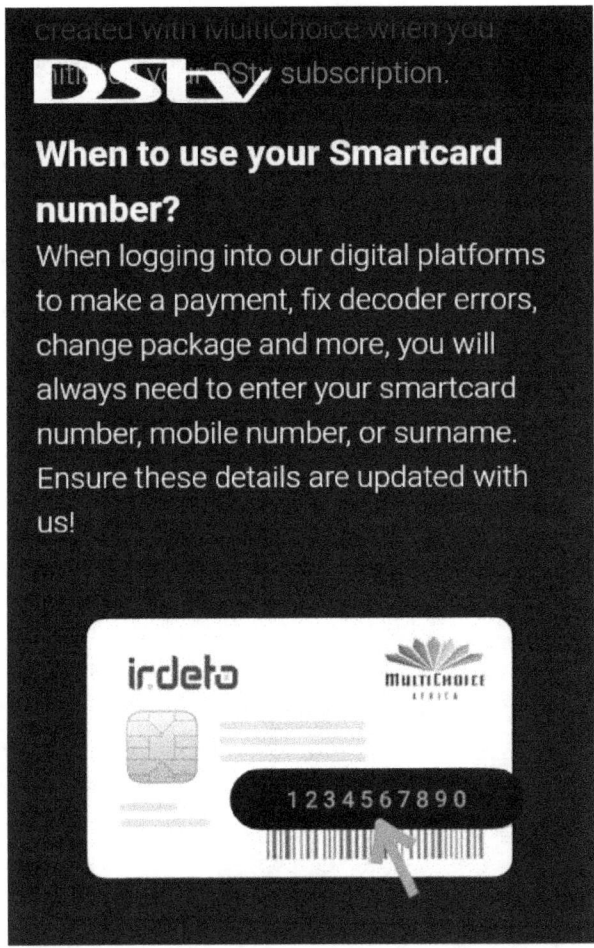

3. **Selar:** Their FAQ is categorized into 3 for different groups, only one is visible with a V sign that shows the other two when clicked on.

Same thing goes for the questions, the answers are embedded in

the + sign seen at the right end of the questions.
Only questions are visible.6

THE FAQ GUIDE

Feel free to email us if you don't find an answer here.

hello@selar.co

For Merchants ⌄

For Merchants

How do I For Affiliates my store? +

For Customers

How do I get paid ? +

When funds are in your wallet, +
withdrawal fees?

Minimum Payout / Withdrawal +
amount?

4.Facebook

First thing I noticed about their FAQ was its simplicity. It started like this:

Help Center : Hi, how can we help you?
- Then a search bar.
- The questions are categorized into 6 boxes.

For each one you click on, there is a vertical list of questions with a V on the right end that contains the answers when you click on it.

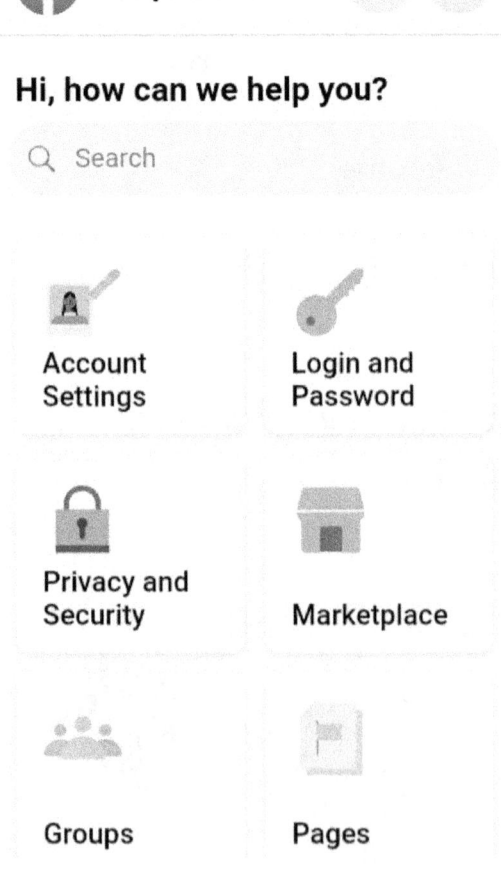

THE FAQ GUIDE

5. Palmers: Took a while but found their FAQ under the category 'company'.

- Boldly titled Frequently Asked Questions.
- Categorize into 9.
- Very simple and accessible.

6. Nivea
- One question I saw in the FAQ was Does Beiersdorf use palm oil or palm kernel oil? This shows that your customers definitely want to know everything.

- This brand made good use of pictures to catch the reader's attention.

7. Pampers
- Use the 'sign that signifies 'help.
- Use embedded links.
- A search bar.

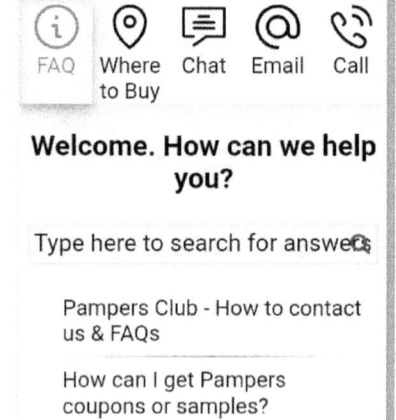

THE FAQ GUIDE

8. Amazon KDP
- Has a lengthy list of categories and questions.(guess,they do not want any loophole).
- The visible questions contains sub categories
- Underneath the Help section is the 'Contact Us' button that says"Can't find your answer in help pages? Contact us.

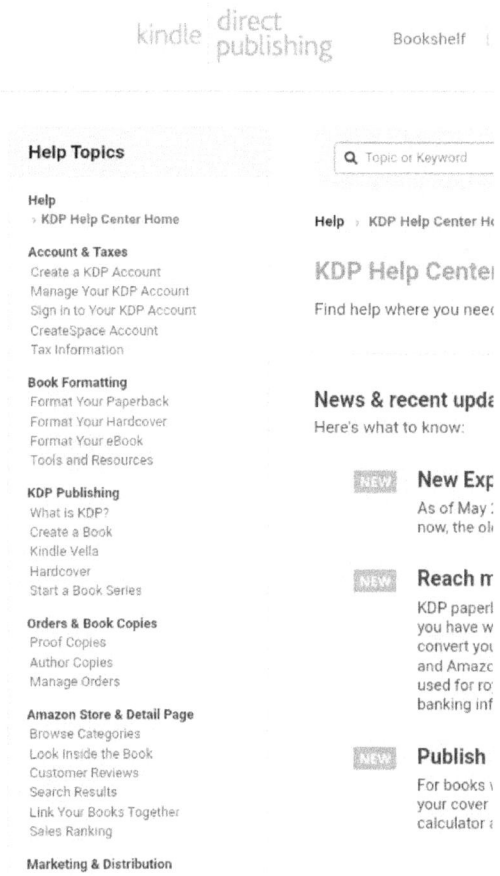

9. Apple
- Titled Apple Support

- Done in classic black and white.
- Categorize neatly.
- Categories are broken into subcategories and answers are well detailed.

Apple Support

THE FAQ GUIDE

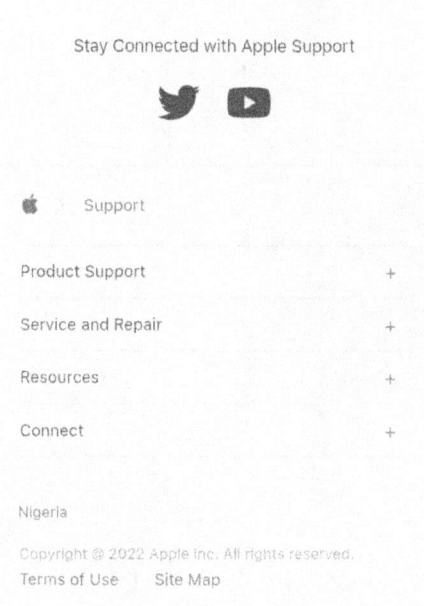

10. **Air Peace**
    - I noticed the FAQ was divided into two: Reservation FAQ Air Peace Advantage {these are probably the areas they get more frequent questions}
    - FAQs are vertically written with only questions visible, the answer comes out when you click on the + sign.

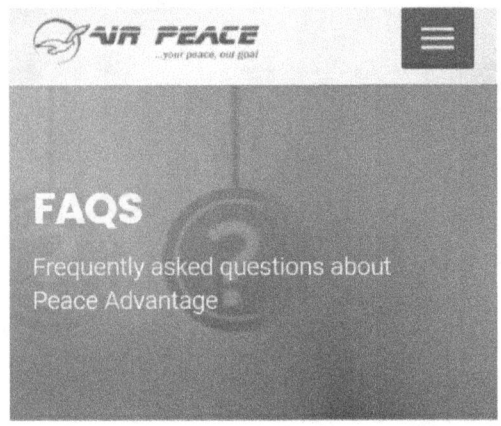

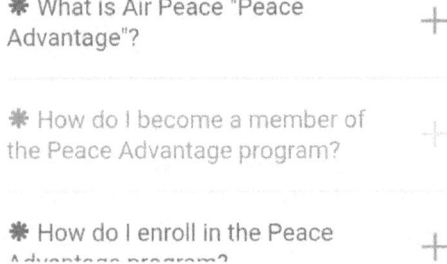

11. Chrisland School
To see their FAQ,you would use the search bar on the home page but once you find it(this is not advisable for a startup or a small business).
- It becomes easy from there,the answers are so detailed that scrolling through their FAQ is taking a trip to the school.
- The categories are highlighted in green boxes.(the color of the school).

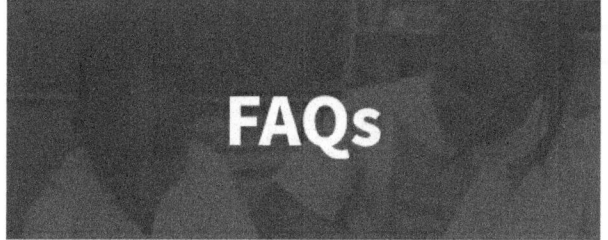
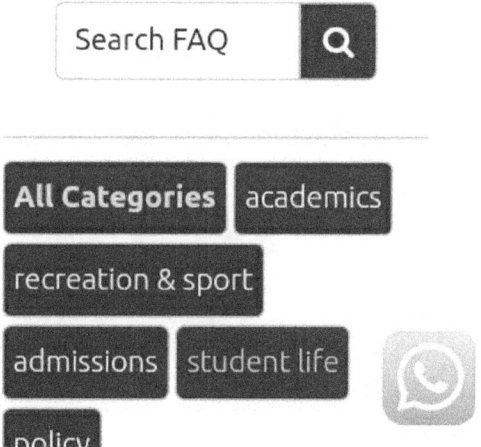

12. Dr Brown's
Customer support--blog--FAQ.
(That's where how I found their FAQ)
- Q&A are written vertically.
- Questions in blue(the brand's color), Answers in black.

- Each answer ends with a blue tab, with the inscription 'Read More' for more details.

13. The Holy See:The Vatican
One intriguing FAQ!
Their FAQ is titled 'Useful Information'.
Heading: How to×2.

Then other information with its sub categories. The FAQ wasn't done in Q&A style but more a directory with embedded

THE FAQ GUIDE

links.
(like we discussed in Chapter.5.
You would also noticed how that made their FAQ short and contained in one page)

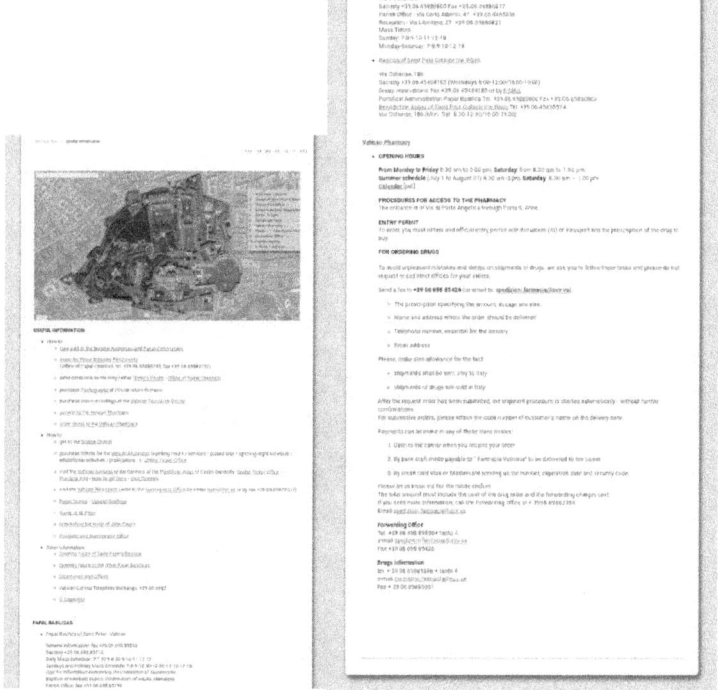

14. Starbucks
Found it as a subcategory under Customer Service.
- Titled 'How can we help you?'
- This is the one of two FAQ in all the 25 here that was numbered (243 Q &A)
- The 'Popular questions' I believe was strategically put at the end so as not to derail the customer.(that way you don't lose the focus on why you came knocking at the FAQ page.
    o

69

Popular Questions

How do I use the Scan Only or Scan & Pay Tabs in the Starbucks Mobile app? – Video Tutorial

How do I get a free coffee on National Coffee Day?

How do I place my Starbucks order using Siri?

How do I check my Starbucks Card balance?

How do I redeem my Birthday Reward? Where can I redeem my Birthday Reward?

- Show more ...

15. Louis Vuitton
- Titled, Can we help you?
- Done in plain and black and white.
- There is a box to email on client services and 'interact with Us' tab and a 'Message us'

16. Spotify
This FAQ is neatly tucked in the 'About us' section.
- Titled help site.
- The Top Solutions"(TS).
- category refers to the most asked questions.

The very basics.

- Ever ready to help with a wide range of options.
- Very catchy color.

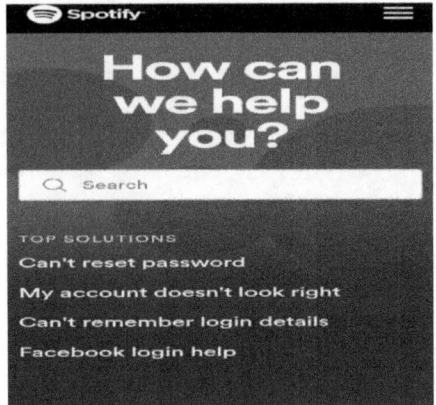

17. Adidas

Adidas puts FREQUENTLY ASKED QUESTIONS in bold capital letters.
- Below that is Support Topics.
- 12 categories
- Easy to see and use.

FREQUENTLY ASKED QUESTIONS

HOW DO I RETURN MY PRODUCT(S)?

WHAT ARE THE TERMS AND CONDITIONS?

WHY CAN'T I FIND MY ORDER IN MY ORDER HISTORY?

WHY DOESN'T MY PROMOTION CODE APPLY THE CORRECT DISCOUNT TO MY ORDER?

HOW DO I CREATE AN ACCOUNT?

WHAT SHOULD I KNOW ABOUT PERSONALIZED GEAR?

18. Google
Who imagined that a search engine would have a Help Center but they do.
We go to Google all the time to get answers to our questions. This is the greatest motivation to get an FAQ.
- Easy to access and straight to the point.
- Search bar.

- The FAQ represented their brand.
- It was just like my everyday Google search.

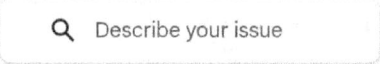

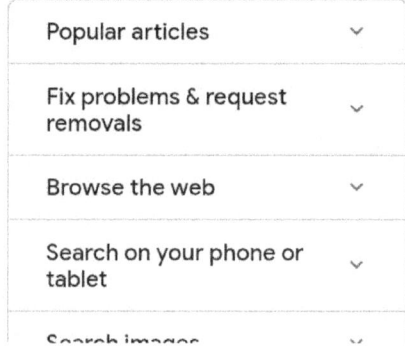

19. WhatsApp
- Titled Help Center
- Has a search bar.
- FAQ is categorized.

THE FAQ GUIDE

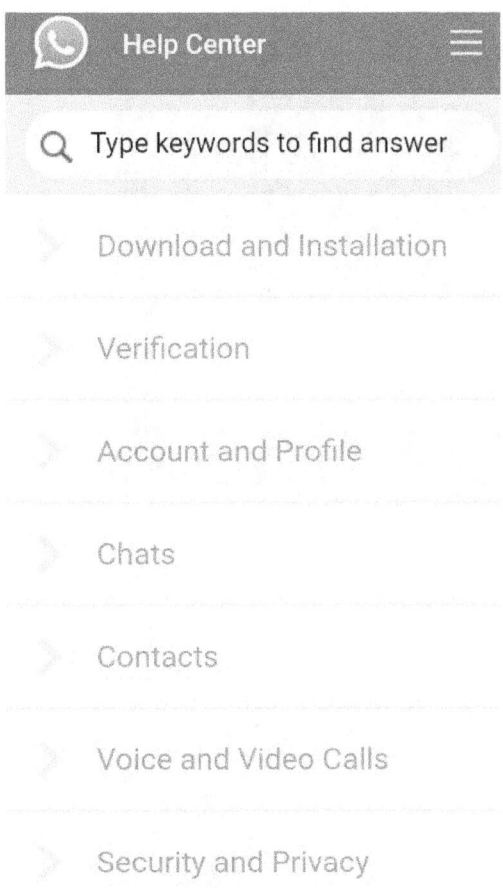

20. Kuda bank
- This FAQ is different.
- Questions were written in purple(the Brand's color).
- Answers are written in blog style, they are called articles.

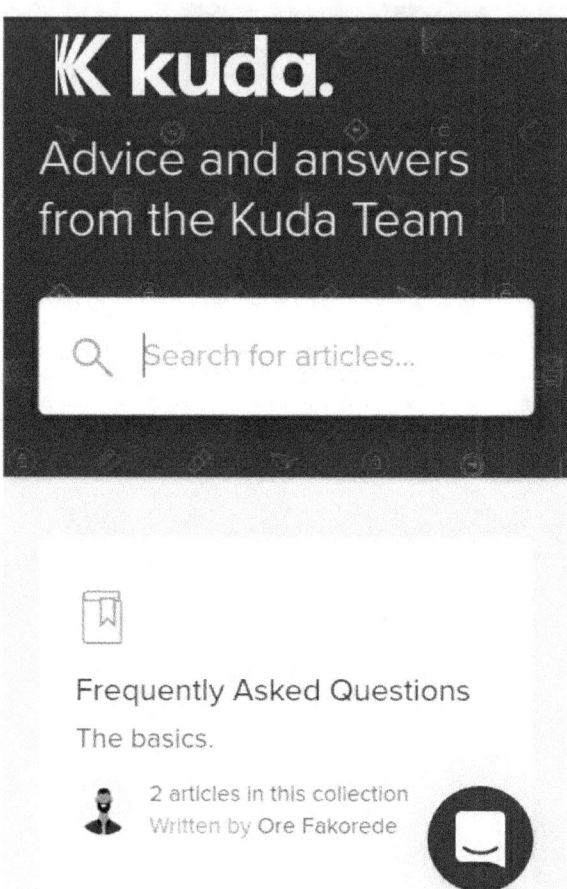

21. Glo
- This FAQ was simply divided into two categories with each having a list of questions.

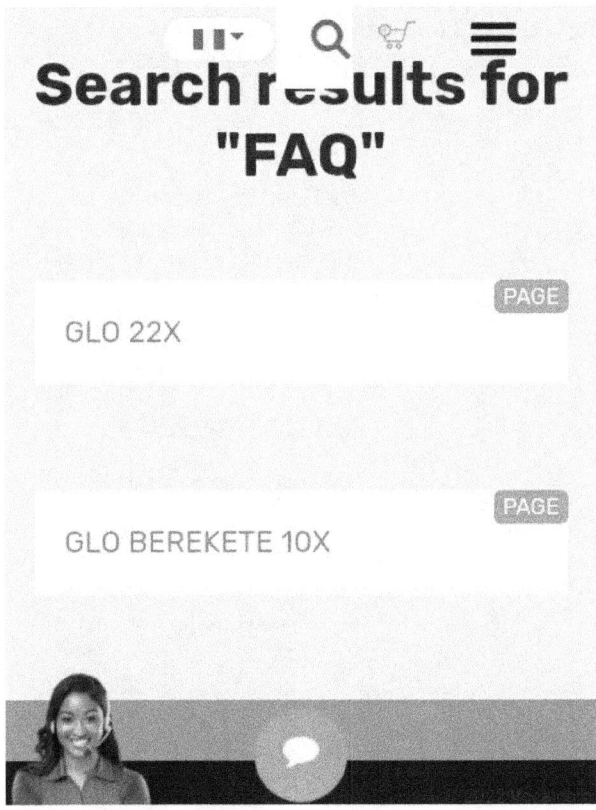

22. Anchor
It is said in Igbo "onye na ju ajuju, à di é fu uzo". It means "he who asks questions does not miss his way".

That is applicable to an FAQ.
When your customers have the information they need, you will get less bad transactions, call out, issues with

customers, returns (product) etc.

- The first thing you see is the light bulb.
- That's what an FAQ is about, it lights your path and shows you the right way.
- The FAQ is titled 'The Complete list'

23. WPS
- Titled "How can we help you"
- Search bar
- Categorize into boxes.
-   Trending topics: classified into 'Basics' and 'Payment issue'.

THE FAQ GUIDE

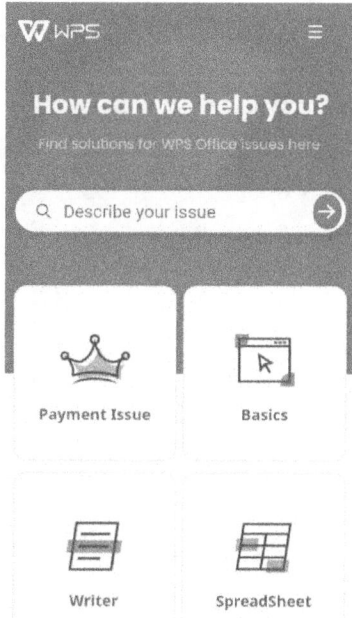

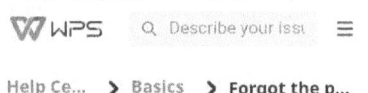

Help Ce... > Basics > Forgot the p...

Forgot the password

Windows Android

Please enter your account on the Sign-in
page, click Forgot on this page, we will send a link to you to reset the password. Please check your inbox.

24. Canva
- Search bar comes first.
- The FAQ was categorized neatly and with icons.
- Top articles come last.
- Even that is split into sub categories.

THE FAQ GUIDE

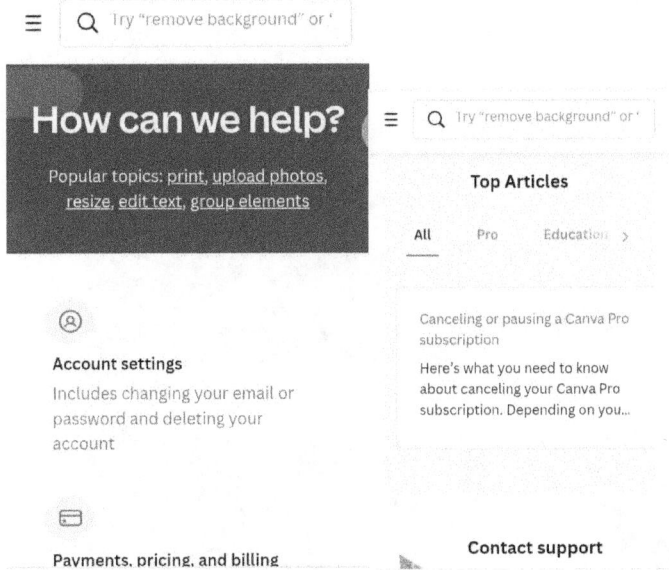

25. Tecno
- Last but not the least is the FAQ with the question mark.
- Bold question mark, beautifully done.
- Has a search bar
- the V sign at the right end of the word "phone" that there is more when you click on it.
- Questions are written in black while answers are done in Ash on a gray background.
- Questions are straight forward,the answers are straight to the point,short,some numbered like a step by step guide.
- Very easy to understand
- Questions only are visible with a '+' sign at the right end,that sign provides the answer when clicked on.
- The invisible answer is a great way to shorten length.

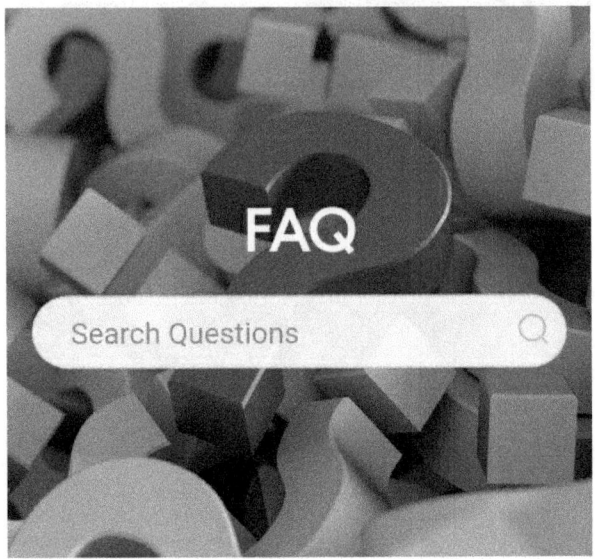

My phone doesn't pre-install the T-band app. How can I use the T-band bracelet? +

Note: No one can predict all the questions your customers would ask so my advice is at the end of your FAQ.
    Make provisions for alternatives i.e.
- Contact us,
- Interact with us,

THE FAQ GUIDE

- Call us,
- Email us.
- Write to us.

CHAPTER 9:REAL FAQ EXAMPLES

The FAQ Guide was borne out of my experience writing FAQs for websites and business. Some of these websites had FAQs but they were poorly written.

Writing FAQ gives me pleasure and opens my mind to the intricacies of each business as I pen down the words.

Here is a compilation of some of the FAQ's written by me, Founder, DNA Imprints.

This should help guide you in writing yours or that of others,be it a website, a business,an event,a book or anything else that needs

1. **DNa Imprints**

   What would you like to know..

Question:What services are offered at DNA Imprints?
Answer:**Here are the services we offer at DNA**

Imprints. We Official letters and emails.
- Speeches Reading in Africa
- FAQ { for websites and businesses}
  - Speech Reading
  - Ghostwriting Biographies/Memoirs
  - Amazon KD Publishing

There are two published books under its DNA Imprints Media.
- Rushed Education.
- The FAQ Guide.

Question: What kind of emails and letters do you write for your clients?
Answer: **DNA Imprints only writes documents so the letters and emails are official.**

Question: Is there a signed document on non-disclosure of the contents of these letters/emails?
Answer: **Discretion is one of our core values at DNA Imprints.**
We understand that the content of a document is confidential so we sign a non disclosure form and we deliver our services based on the content of this agreement.
No one beside the writer of the documents gets a peek at its content.

Question: Does DNA Imprints have the copyrights to these documents (letters, emails written by them?
Answer: **Oh yes! There is something known as Intellectual property and an offense called Plagiarism. The content of any documents written by DNA Imprints falls under the IP and**

Having paid for a job,you get value for that particular job but on no account should our work be copied and used for other purposes.
That would be Intellectual property theft.

Question: What sort of refund policy do you have in place at DNA Imprints?
Answer: **Besides our published works,'The Rushed Education' and 'The FAQ Guide'**
DNA Imprints is purely a digital service provider.
Here is what guarantees you a 100% refund.
- **Paying for the wrong subscription.**
- **When DNA Imprints does not meet up with the deadline,without a good reason and prior notice to the client.**
- **Money paid for a service,DNA Imprints doesn't and can't offer.**

Question: Is ghost Writing a part of what you do at DNA Imprints?
Answer : **No,we do not offer Ghostwriting services at DNA Imprints for now. Provisions for GW would be made in the future.**

Question:How does DNA Imprints charge, by pages, monthly subscription or one job at a time?
Answer: **Most of the services offered by DNA Imprints are one-offs but bespoke services can extend for longer.i.e weekly, monthly or more.**
- **Services like Audiobook Narration, Editing & Proofreading are charged based on pages.**
- **FAQ, Adverts & Amazon KDP uploads have one-off charges.**
- **While Speech writing & Speech Presentation**

are premium so charged based on service,client needs, preferences & audience.

Question: The advert by DNA Imprints, does that include advert placement?
Answer: **oh no, We don't do advert placement.**
DNA Imprints only writes the words that make up the advert.

Question: What's 5yy is the number of questions and answers that make up an FAQ pack?
Answer: **DNA Imprints has 3 FAQ packs.**
- **Silver {15 Q &A}**
- **Gold {30 Q &A}**
- **Platinum {60 Q &A}**
- **Updates**
- **Custom pack{additional 6 Q&A}**
- **Pictorial/FAQ.**

Question: How much does your service cost?
Answer : At DNA Imprints,every service is unique,so the prices differ .
Here is a list of our books & services and their prices.
To buy a copy of Rushed Education:

https://selar.co/4hox

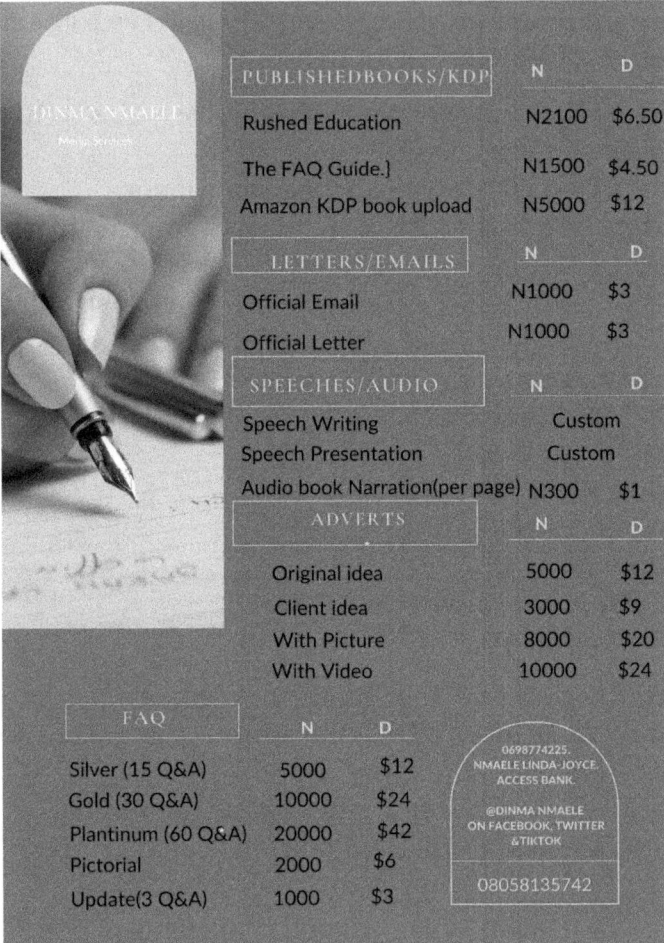

Question: Is there an extra charge for updates done on the FAQ for returning clients?

Answer: Yes! A token, only for returning clients whose FAQ was written on their own. Updates are done regularly so it's a pack of its own.

Question: An FAQ is mainly found in websites, do you design websites too?

Answer: No we don't, DNA Imprints writes only the questions and answers that make up the FAQ page/section of your website.

Question: Is there a customized FAQ pack where I can decide on the number of questions and answers I want?
Answer: DNA Imprints has a custom FAQ pack for clients who want more than the number of questions & answers in any of the three packs.
6 extra Q &A (2000).

Question: Are your FAQ simply written as a list of questions and answers?
Answer : FAQ done in words are written in Q &A style. DNA Imprints offers FAQ in pictorial and video form.

Question: What is the difference between editing and proofreading?
Answer:
Editing involves a process to improve the overall quality of writing by enhancing flow, readability and structure of a written work.
Proofreading is the correcting of surface errors such as grammar, spelling and punctuation. This is the final stage of editing.

Question: Does DNA Imprints offer both services?
Answer: Yes, we do!

Question: Where is DNA Imprints Media located.?
Answer: DNA Imprints is located at Abuja but operates fully online.
You can reach DNA Imprints through:
- Facebook: DNA Imprints Nmaele or simply click here

- nmaeleDNA Imprints@gmail.com
- WhatsApp or Call :08058135742.

Digital Services can be delivered anywhere in the world. Books are available on Selar @

Location: Abuja

Maths Hub {A Maths homework assistance program and tutoring}.

Ask me anything!

Question: As the name implies, is Maths all you do at Maths Hub?

Answer: Oh Yes! Maths Hub was created to solve the Maths problems of kids in Middle School /Junior Secondary School.

Although, there is still in the future, that Maths Hub would expand to include other subjects (science based).

Question: What services do you offer at Maths Hub?
Answer : At Maths Hub, we offer two major services.
- Private/Group Maths Tutoring.{1 hour, 30 minutes | 3×weekly}
- Maths Homework Assistance{MHA}.

Question: How does the MHA work?
Answer: Monthly subscribers are to send a snapshot of the homework to Whatsapp on 07068280202 before 5pm.

Snapshots of Workings and Answers will be sent back, alongside audio recordings to further explain the Problem before 7pm daily.

Question: Who can subscribe to your service?
Answer:

Question : Do you sell Mathematical products ?
Answer : Maths Hub is a service based business.
We can only recommend,endorse and give discount coupons for certain brands selling products like Maths sets,books,graphs etc.

Question: What topics in Maths does Maths Hub cover?
Answer: Maths Hub tackles Mathematical problems ranging from Whole Numbers, Fractions, Estimation,Computer Application,Open Sentences,Algebra,Angles, Statistics,,Decimal Number, Multiples,Ratio,Square,Data, Simple Measuration, Family Arithmetic,Rates & Proportion, Revision & Preparation for Junior WAEC.

Question: Is subscription one time or monthly?
Answer : Our services are based on monthly subscriptions at Maths Hub.

Question: What is the refund policy on subscription?
Answer: At Maths Hub, we understand everyone wants their money's worth so we have come up with a system that is beneficial to both parties.
Here are some possible scenario for a a refund:
- In the case where a subscriber pays for a monthly service,then falls ill after a few days and doesn't come back for a period of 3 weeks -1 month.
- When a subscriber overpays.
- When a subscriber pays and doesn't attend a single class,but with prior notice to Maths Hub.
- When a client subscribes to a wrong service. Example: when a client pays for tutoring instead of homework assistance.

Question: Does Maths hub have a scheduled time for homework support and tutorial?
Answer: The MHA is scheduled between 5pm-7pm.
Homework should be sent before 5pm and answers delivered on or before 7pm.
Monday to Friday.

While private /group Math tutoring is between 1 hour. 30 minutes,3 times a week.

Question: How does the Maths Hub operate?
Answer: The Maths Hub tutoring can be in three levels.
- Beginner: Introduction to Junior Secondary School Mathematics.
- Intermediate:JSS2-3
- Proficient: Revision for JSS3 WAEC.

These can be divided into
- Private: Maths tutoring for one subscriber.
- Group:10-12 subscribers per level.

Group tutoring is encouraged to Foster learning and healthy competition between our teens.

Question: Where is the Maths hub located?
Answer: There are no physical locations for now. Maths Hub operates online only.

Question: What online platform does Maths hub use for its services?
Answer: Maths Hub uses the WhatsApp platform for MHA programs.
The learning aids in the form of audio, screenshots,video etc are uploaded to a closed private group and access is granted to subscribers to help refresh their memory.

Question: How can I reach Maths Hub?
Answer: You can reach on **07068280202** {Call or WhatsApp}
like and follow our Facebook page @Mathshub. Send us a mail:
Mathshub22@gmail.com.

www.printhouse.ng

Hello, how can we help?

Q: What products/services do you offer?
A: We print on the following:
Labels & Stickers (the Stickers comes in round & square shapes)
Clothing: Tees, Polo shirts, Caps, Beanies Visor, Hoods & Sweatshirts.
Business Stationery: Business Cards, Letterheads, Continuation Sheets, Plastic ID cards, Branded Envelopes, Brochures & Leaflets.
Events: Paper Bags, Large Format Banner, Souvenir, Flyers & Handbills, Custom Mug, Calendar, Notepad & Jotter.
Wall Art.

Q: What is Wall Art?
A: Wall Art is a type of decoration ranging from canvases to framed prints. Ours is a custom gallery wrap canvas frame and its uses are endless ranging from a personalized gift to loved ones to being used as a wall frame in an organization for Mission/Vision Statement to family goals or to print words of affirmation or a verse from a Holy Book.

Q: What does it look like & how fast can it be delivered?
A: Our Wall Art is printed on high-end scratch resistant ink-jet machines using the best quality poly-cotton canvas material. It is delivered in 3 days framed with a beautiful lightweight wooden frame.

Q: What is the difference between a Continuation Sheet and a Letterhead?
A: Continuation Sheet is a simpler carrying just a Logo and brand ensuring anyone with a copy sees & has your identity/brand at heart. While a Letterhead is the heading at the top of a sheet of letter paper. This heading contains the name, address, logo or corporate design and sometimes has a background pattern.

FAQ {BODY SAFETY}

Q: What does the Body Safety Academy do?
A: Body Safety Academy uses a comprehensive, research focused and evidence based strategies to equip children with the knowledge and skills to prevent sexual abuse.

We do this in two ways;

1. **Educate the children directly.**
2. **Educate parents, guardians, teachers and child advocates who in turn enlighten children.**

It has the following programmes;

1. **Email course.**
2. **Audio course.**
3. **Whatsapp/ Telegram classes.**
4. **One on one coaching.**
5. **Group coaching.**
6. **School training.**

7. Zoom training.
8. Workshop facilitation.

Q: Do you discuss sex while teaching Body Safety?
A: Body safety is suited for children aged 7 months to 9 years, we do not discuss sex. We rather make the children aware of sexual abuse, harmful situations and teach them strategies to equip them against sexual abuse using appropriate terms.

Q: What age is okay for a parent to bring up the topic 'Body Safety'?
A: One of the modules in our body safety program is 'body parts awareness and appreciation' that is learning the proper names of your body parts which could be started before a baby turns one.

This is evidence based and can work for any willing parent. A child can be taught to gradually spot his or her body parts as early as 7 months without speaking.

Q: How do I assure my child that it's okay to open up about a 'near harmful situation'?
A: At Body Safety Academy we encourage openness through proper communication. Every child should be able to express himself or herself at home or anywhere else without fear.

A child that is constantly shut down cannot be outspoken for obvious reasons. These children will lack confidence and will most likely be frightened of you.

Children petrified of their parents or guardians will not disclose a 'near harmful situation or an incident of sexual abuse'.

You should answer these questions;

1. Is my child afraid of me?
2. Do they trust me?
3. Have I encouraged them to be fully expressive?

4. Do I spend sufficient time with them?
5. Can they say 'I love them'?
6. Have I ever accused them without hearing their own side of the story?
7. Has my behavior in recent times made them doubt my love?
8. Am I impatient with them?

If you have laid the proper foundation, your children will come to you without you asking. What is this 'proper foundation'? To know, you'd have to take our courses.

Q: At what age should my kids stop taking their bath together?
A: Same sex can take their bath together but with the supervision of a parent, until the time you feel they can bathe themselves individually and when they get to that age, it's imperative they bathe alone. Females and males must have their baths differently.

Q: At what age should a parent stop (un)dressing before their kids?
A: At two (2)

Q: Do I have to ask for permission to kiss my child?
A: Yes, it is a simple way of teaching consent and boundaries.

Q: What is the difference between body safety and sex education?
A: Body safety education is a standardized teaching that aims to equip the child with protective strategies to prevent sexual abuse. The words, descriptions, pictures and examples are age appropriate, at the end of the education children become knowledgeable about their rights, consent, boundaries and proper actions to take to protect themselves in harmful situations.

Sex education is the provision of knowledge about sex, sexuality and relationships. It helps kids make informed

decisions about their sexuality, physical and emotional health.

Q: Is child sexual abuse only committed by adults?
A: No, there is also 'peer on peer sexual abuse' which is also called child on child sexual abuse.

One third of child sexual abuse is carried out by under 18s (Report by StopItNow UK).

Q: If I teach my child about body safety won't it predispose them to danger?
A: It does the opposite. Body safety education arms every child that is enlightened. They will learn different strategies that'd protect them from being sexually abused.

Q: Do we have a functional Child Protective Service in Nigeria?
A: Yes

Q: What institutions are available to protect the child?

A: 1. Sexual assault referral centres (SARC).
   2. National Agency for prohibition of traffic in persons and other related matters (NAPTIP).

Q: What is grooming?
A: It is the process whereby a pedophile befriends a child to form an emotional connection so trust is formed, consequently making it easier for sexual exploitation to occur.

Q: Will body safety spoil my child?
A: No. It will rather arm your child with protective strategies needed to prevent sexual abuse.

Q: Is it possible for a parent to ignorantly stimulate their own child sexually?

A: Yes. Unfortunately, parents have and continue to ignorantly abuse their children sexually.

Most times it occurs during bath, dressing or play time. There have been reported cases where parents arouse their young children.

Q: How do I contact the Body Safety Academy?
bodysafetyacademy@gmail.com
Whatsapp: +2348085432505

Beyond Bullying{BB}
What you should know.

- What does Beyond Bullying stand for?
- What inspired the Beyond Bullying movement?
- Who is eligible to join?
- What are the benefits of being a part of the Beyond Bullying movement?
- How can they send in their stories?
- How do I get a copy of the Beyond Bullying Journal?

https://www.fiverr.com/s2/b0bf63e45a

FAQ- Learn about us!

Question: What packages are available?

I offer 3 WordPress website design packages.
BASIC: One Page website with 3 Sections or 3-page website or blog, STANDARD: website with up to 6 pages, and PREMIUM: A website with responsive design, up to 10 pages with eCommerce.
Kindly send me a message so I can give you a custom offer.

Q: Do you use pre-made templates, or do you build from scratch?

I believe all websites are different, so on every project, I build from scratch. This is to enable me tailor the website to your brand and niche. If you have a custom suggestion, kindly let me know. Send me a message.

Q: Do you handle hosting, or does the client need to purchase their own hosting plan?

Choosing a good hosting provider is essential to your website. Hosting plays a huge role in determining the page speed and security of your entire website. You need to purchase hosting on your own because of its recurring payments. However, I can guide you in making the best decision.

Q: How fast will it take to complete the project?

Each WordPress Website design package has its delivery time ranging from 3-10 days, and I deliver at the stipulated time. However, if you'd like your project finished and delivered faster, send me a message right away, and I'll see if I can make it possible.

Q: Are the stock images used in designing the website provided by a client or, can you provide stock images of your own?

I provide free stock images to suit the pages, But if you'd like your own photos, Send them over, and I'll use them on your WordPress website.

Q: Will my website be mobile-friendly?

Since the start of 2021, mobile traffic has consistently accounted for more than half of the total website traffic worldwide. (54.8%). So I work hard to ensure that all websites I build look great and function perfectly on tablet and mobile devices.

Q: What is SEO, and how does it work?

SEO simply stands for Search Engine Optimization. By optimizing the pages and content of your website to satisfy your clients' search intent, the Search engines will rank your website higher. More views means visibility and more sales.

Q: How will SEO help my business visibility/growth?

Well, As a business owner, optimizing your websites for search engines is the best decision you'll ever make, as organic traffic is essential for your business growth and ROI.

Q: Will I be able to update my site myself when it's finished?

Yes! I love when my clients take control of their website and learn to manage it on their own. A comprehensive PDF manual that will enable you to take control of your website will be made available to you. I am also open to questions regarding your WordPress Website Before and after your project is complete.

Q: Are there bonus offers?

For WordPress Website design, I offer 10% off on your first order

Q: Can I contact you outside the Fiverr app?

No, sorry, it's against the rules. However, I'm a native English speaker, and I promise that communication will be smooth and precise.

http://www.kashglobal-ng.com

Get Help!

Q : What services does Kash Global Venture(KGV) offer?

KGV offers the following services

PROCUREMENT & SHIPMENT(together)

SUPPLIER PAYMENT

We ensure we help pay your suppliers in record time(one business day)

SHIPPING

You can ship goods into Nigeria through KGV by sending it via our office in China.

PROCUREMENT

KGV eases the burden of travel expenses,erases the fear of fraudulent purchases from China by buying the items you want from China and ensuring it gets to you here in Nigeria.

E-COMMERCE

Q : Is there a limit to the size of items KGV can ship in / out?

The word limit is an excuse in KGV and that is not acceptable. We ship items as small as 0.25 and as mighty as can fit in a container.

Q : Does KGV deliver within the country also and to how many states?

KGV delivers to every habitable corner of the country.

Q : Is China the only country KGV ships goods from?

Currently, KGV ships only from China.

Q : For a client outside the zone where KGV is physically located, what steps can be taken if they require the services of KGV?

While the major service KGV provides is shipping items into the country (Nigeria), we deem it fit to ease the minds of our clients who are outside our physical zone by using the services of our partners(local delivery services) to get their goods to them.

Q : Can KGV serve logistics needs of a client through its partners?

KGV cares about the accessibility of our services to our clients so we encourage our clients to reach out to us through our listed partners by sending their goods via those partners to our warehouse in China and we will deliver here in Nigeria.

THE FAQ GUIDE

Q : Does KGV have an insurance policy to cover for delayed delivery or loss of items caused by either a sunk ship or air crash or road accident?

The insurance policy of KGV states that 5% of the total amount of goods will be refunded in such unfortunate circumstances.

Q : Are there specific items KGV can procure and ship in?

KGV can ship anything and everything. From liquid batteries to phones, fashion accessories to furniture or cars. KGV has got you covered.

Kashkiddies
What you need to know!

Q : What does Kash Kiddies do?
Kash Kiddies is a company that sells and distributes children's clothes, mostly wholesale.

Q : Does Kash Kiddies source its clothes locally?
All of the Kash Kiddies wear are from a Saudi Arabian company, HIBOBI FASHION.

Q : What other age group does Hibobi Fashion cater for?
The Hibobi Fashion caters to the clothing needs of children aged 0-12.

Q : Can a client buy something else not under the category of kids wear from Hibobi Fashion through Kash Kiddies.
Yes, the Hibobi Fashion is a complete children store, they sell clothes, shoes and toys.

At the request of a customer, these things can be purchased.

Q : What is the quantity of minimum order?
While Kash Kiddies is a major distributor catering to wholesalers, a retailer who wants to enjoy the same benefits but cannot buy our minimum order quantity can buy at least 30 pieces.

Q : Is there a physical walk-in show room for Kash Kiddies or it only has presence online?
Kash Kiddies is both an online and offline store.
Our warehouse is at : 26, Ipodo street by oriyomi street Ikeja Lagos.

Kash Kiddies can be found on
Facebook: @Kash Kiddes
Instagram : @KiddiesKash

Q : What is the time frame for delivery at Kash Kiddies?
Delivery in the state of our physical store is almost immediately, whether you are coming to buy at our store or we are delivering it to your doorstep.

EVON FOODS

Explore!

Q: What is Evon foods and who is the story behind it?
The name EVON stands for
E - Everything
O - Organic &
N - Natural.
It was conceived in April 2020 during the lockdown and was launched on 18th July 2020.

This was also the motivation behind the e-book 'Even from the Kitchen' written by the brain and muscle behind EVON Foods, Mrs. Joy Nobis, about her personal story as a housewife who beat the odds and is running a profitable business from her Kitchen.

The book is available for 1499 on Selar. co/evenfromthekitchen.

Q: What products do EVON foods sell?

EVON Foods produces and sells
◆◆Pap(7 variants)
■Ginger Pap (infused with dates)
■Tigernut Pap (infused with dates)
■Nutty Pap (is made of a rich blend of nuts)
■Coconutty Pap (infused with dates)
■Baby 3-in-1 Pap.
■Millet pap (infused with dates)
■Soy pap (is blended with soybeans and nuts)

◆◆Tombrown (a rich blend of more than 8 grains).
■Baby Tombrown
■Adult Tombrown

◆◆Swallow
■Oat Mixed Swallow (good for Diabetics)
■Mixed Grain Swallow.

Q: What sizes are available?

EVON Pap comes in three sizes
500g, 1kg, and Custard(paint) bucket.

EVON Tom brown comes in three sizes
500g, 1kg, and Custard(paint)bucket.

EVON Swallow comes in 2 sizes
1.2kg and Custard(paint) bucket.

Q: Can you offer customized grains at the customer's request?
Ans: Yes.

Q: Does EVON pap come in powdery or fermented frozen form?
Ans: Only in fermented form for now, but will soon start the powered pap.

Q: Do you offer premium service and express delivery:
Ans: Yes.

Q: Do EVON foods cater only to the food needs of the local populace?
Ans: No. Is for everybody.

Q: Are your grains & nuts locally sourced?
Ans: Yes.

Q: What are your payment options.
Ans: Via Transfer or Cash.

Q: What grains/ nuts are infused in your pap and what is the ratio per serving?
Ans: Corn, Millet, Guinea corn, Tigernut, Groundnuts, cashew nuts, Dates.
Ratio: 2:1

Q: Available payment options?
Ans: Acct no: 0428118858. Joy Nobis Adanna. Gtbank.

Q: Is payment on delivery an option?
Ans: Yes.

Q: What age bracket does EVON Foods cater for?
Ans: from 6 months babies to senior citizens.

Babies from 6 months can take our Baby 3-in-1 Pap, Nutty Pap, and BabyTombrown for babies allergic to soy and nuts, we recommend our 3-in-1 Baby Pap.

While our Tigernut, Coconutty pap, and Ginger Pap, Millet pap are recommended for babies up to 8 months because of the ginger taste.

Adults who are not allergic to nuts and soya can take any of the Pap variants, Adult Tombrown, and Swallows.

Magnet Media
Help Topics

Q: What services does Magnet Media group offer?

Magnet Media is a media outfit that specializes in graphic designs and advertisement.
Our designs are done in top notch creativity as you will see on our business page:

We do advertisement on platforms such as
��Facebook and Instagram.

��Billboards

��On Air and Radio

We also manage social media pages for people.

Q: What is the available size of booklets,cards, brochures,banners & leaflets?
A: Magnet Media has it's client's at heart,so we deliver

our services based on our client's request.
All sizes are available.
If a client can think of it, Magnet Media can create it and deliver.

Q: Does Magnet Media group design books?
A: Magnet Media designs and print books too.

Q: What advertising services does the Magnet Media group offer?

A: At Magnet Media, our services include graphic designs, printing and advertising.
We offer sponsored adverts, billboard advert and On Air Adverts.

Q: How long does it take to complete an order?

A: At Magnet Media, payment validates orders.
As soon as payment is made, we start working on your order and we deliver within a day or two.

Q: Does Magnet Media charge for a design and printing separately?

A: Magnet Media charges for designing and printing separately.
This is because of the complexities involved in designing, use of time too.

Also not all clients need the hard (printed) copy of a design.

Q: Is Magnet Media able to deliver Nationwide or does your company use the services of the print house in locations that are not your base?

A: Magnet Media delivers Nationwide, however delivery time may vary based on the location.

Q: What are the procedures Magnet Media uses in planning an advertising campaign?

A: Here is a step by step outline, Magnet Media follows for a successful advertising campaign.

��Step 1: Creating a page.

��Step 2: Post in content.

��Step 3: Employ the services of a professional page manager.

��Step 4: Boost a post.

��Step 5: Input your card details and how many days or weeks you want your advert to run.

��Step 6: Run your advert.

Q: What packages do you offer under your advertising campaign?

A: Packages include:

��Graphics designing .

��Logo (if there is none).

��Facebook advert on my Offical page and official instagram page.

Q: What is the coverage range(location & audience) for the On Air campaign done by Magic Media?

A: Our adverts range and audience for On air adverts is

55 countries.

Q: What locations do your billboard advert cover?
A: Lagos
Imo
Aba
Port Harcourt

Q: How long does it take for results to show and are there follow ups?

A: the results for sponsored adverts is immediately

Billboard adverts: 2-3 days

On air: 2-3 days
Magnet Media takes care of the follow up.

Q: Is there an insurance policy to cover for when a billboard is damaged?

A: Magnet Media is not liable to pay for damages on a billboard used for advertising because the billboard belongs to a third-party.

Q: Is DSTV & MYTV the only licensed TV stations within the reach of Magnet?

A: DSTV and MYTV have audiences in 55 countries with millions of viewers within their reach and advertisement is a game of numbers.
However, they are not the only licensed TV station within our reach.

Q: What is the number of their audience?

A: They have millions of viewers but how far an advert

goes depends on how long it plays On air, how many weeks(for sponsored adverts) and how many months (for on air and billboard adverts) as the cases may be

Q: Does Magnet Media give discount offers for returning clients?

A: Magnet Media offers discounts for returning clients.

Q: How Magnet Media charge for advertising campaigns, per advert or the entire campaign?

A: In the case of an advertising campaign, Magnet Media charges for the entire campaign.

Q: How do I contact Magnet Media?
A: You can teach us via WhatsApp on 09015931024 or send us a mail @ geofferyjeffery7@gmail.com.

The book 'Rushed Education' by DNA Imprints Nmaele.
Ask me anything!

Q: What is double promotion?
A: Simply put, this is a practice of taking a child, one class further than the next class they should actually be in.
For example: Moving a child from Grade 4-Grade 6 instead of Grade 5 based on his or her good Academic result.
Q: Does it still happen in schools?
A: At the time this book was published. It still happens.

Q: Does the Author believe things may have panned out differently for her if her education wasn't rushed?

A: DNA Imprints truly believes that a lot of what she went through could be avoided.

    I.   The bullying won't have happened in the first place. She would have gone to boarding school a lot more prepared (emotionally & mentally). A lot of the bullying was as a result of her being the youngest in her class.

    II.   The entire bad experience in boarding school; the inability to care properly for herself, to speak up for herself etc could have been avoided.

    III.   She had always been drawn to arts but the sciences won't have been as difficult for her to process as it was then.

    IV.   Choosing a career path won't have taken so long because her strengths would shine so brightly that the pathway is clear.

Q: What aspects of DNA Imprints's life were mostly affected, social, physiological or her Academics?

A: All parts were affected. DNA Imprints went into secondary school with quite a high dose of self confidence and esteem but her experience in boarding school changed her.

Her self-image suffered from the constant taunting and name calling. From being called a pig to being called possessed by evil spirits. Making and keeping friends was hard too. By the time her Academics joined the list. It became a question of "Is there anything that girl is good at?"

Q: Is writing this book a long time dream achieved, and what does the Author hope to achieve with this book?
A: No, the idea to write this book was borne out of the pain DNA Imprints felt when she noticed two of her pupils struggling like she did. One of them is really smart but can't seem to cope because he was being rushed through school.
DNA Imprints believed that sharing her story with their parents would change their hearts and prompt them to take a step back for the sake of their children. DNA Imprints never had the opportunity to speak with them. Hopefully this book does that on a larger scale.

Q: What is the Author's objective in writing this story?
A: To inform and educate people on the consequences of Rushed Education.
This book would break the barrier, one child at a time and no other child has to go through what DNA Imprints experienced.

Q: Has the Author written other books?
A: Yes; DNA Imprints has three works set to be published this year.
        i.   The FAQ Guide.
        ii. The Beyond Bullying Journal {BBJ}
The BBJ is a Journal created for students to document their experiences in school. It is designed using the

school calendar, with tips on how to deal with bullying, body safety etc...

   iii. Chétà {a Memoir}.

https://ofinglobal.com.ng/

Q: What products and services does Ofin Global Engineering offer?

A: We design, supply and install various capacities and types of cold room facilities. These Cold Room come in three package:

•The Freezer Cold Storage Room
This is a minus temperature storage Cold Room.

• Chest Cold Room
A positive temperature Cold Room.

•Blast Freezer Processing Room
This is a special Cold Room designed for extreme temperatures as low as -30° - 40°.

▫Ofin Global Engineering is also one of the major local representatives of various global PU Panel companies here in Nigeria.

We supply quality European standard PU Panels of various sizes and thickness ranging from 50mm, 100mm, 120mm, 150mm.
Our Panel density is 42 kg/m3.

▫We supply quality brands of industrial refrigeration

equipments of various sizes like;

- Compressors (Copeland, Bitzer, Dorin, Maneurop)
- Condensing Units
- Evaporator Units
- Cold room doors and other cold room accessories.

Q : Does Ofin Global Engineering offer only design, supply and installation of Cold Room?
A: Ofin Global Engineering is keen on durability, reliability and sustainability of your cold room facilities.
So we offer periodic routine maintenance service called Annual maintenance Contract (AMC)
AMC : The AMC (Annual Maintenance Contract) covers maintenance services of refrigeration units as per refrigeration unit recommendations, maintenance consumables, all breakdown repairs.

Q : What does HVAC&R stand for?

A: Heating Ventilation and Air Conditioning & Refrigerator.

Q: What is the difference between a Freezer Cold Storage, a Chiller cold room and a Blast Freezer Processing Room?
A: •The Freezer Cold Storage Room
Cold Room whose operating temperature could range between -5^0c to -20^0c depending on the product's

storage temperature.

Mostly the Cold Room types are used in the storage of Frozen Foods, Meats and the likes.

- Chiller Cold Room on the other hand is a Positive Temperature Cold Room whose operating temperature could range between 0^0c to 18^0c also depending on the products storage temperature. These Cold Room types are used in the storage of Fruits, Vegetables, Dairies, Pharmaceutical Products and the likes.
- Blast Freezers are Processing Cold Rooms (i.e. not meant for product storage). The Blast freezers operates at extremely low temperature ranges of -35^0c and below.

This type of cold rooms are mostly used by the farmers for the processing of their freshly slaughtered poultry products before storage in the freezer cold room to maintain the temperature. They are also used in the ice cream processing factories.

Q: Does Ofin Global Engineering offer installation and supply of Cold Room storage facilities.

A : YES we do.

At Ofin Global Engineering our major field of expertise is the design and installation of Cold Room Storage facilities of different capacities and temperatures.

We design and install Positive Temperature Cold Rooms (for fruits and vegetables), Negative Temperature Cold Rooms (for Frozen foods and the likes), we also design Blast Freezer Machines for the fast freezing of freshly slaughtered Poultry Products, Ice Cream products and like products requiring extremely low temperature range (-35 degree cent) for processing.

Q : What does HVAC&R stand for?

A: The acronym HVAC&R stands for Heat Ventilation Air Conditioning and Refrigeration.

Q: Does Ofin Global Engineering offer an option to hire a Cold Room storage facility for a short period of time?

A: YES. We have partners who are into the cold room business of leasing out their cold room facilities at a reasonable fee for an agreed period of time.

Q: Considering the size of a Cold Room, can Ofin Global Engineering install in other states asides Lagos State?

A: We are not limited by size in our designs and installation, in fact we design according to your specified requirement and available resources.

Most of our cold rooms are built on the client's facility. We procure all needed equipment and material and deploy them to the clients location, where the installation and assembling is carried out within an estimated period of time.

Q: How large is a Cold Room and how much space should a prospective buyer budget?

A: A cold room can be as large as a football field, or as your standard room.

The size and budget of the cold room is majorly determined by the client's products requirement i.e. the capacity of products he wants to store in the cold room.

You can check out the price list page for various capacities and prices of cold rooms.

Q: Can Ofin Global Engineering provide a Cold Room that can switch between a Freezer Cold Storage and Blast Freezer Processing Room?

A: NO. Every cold room is built specifically for its usage.

The Blast freezer design is totally different from the freezer cold room design.

For instance,the Blast freezer is designed to operate at a much lower temperature than the cold room and in these designs much more heavy equipment and materials are used which in turn attracts more cost to build.

Q: How long does it take for Ofin Global Engineering to complete an installation?

A: Depending on the capacity of the Cold Room to be installed, but for a standard cold room size (say like 15 Tons) our delivery time is 14 days.

Q: If a client needs a storage facility for off season produce like seeds, grains, potatoes, chillies etc.

Can Ofin Global Engineering provide that?

A: YES we can. The storage facility needed for these types of produce are positive temperature cold rooms constantly regulated at the products storage temperature range.

Q: Are bespoke and custom Cold Rooms available at Ofin Global Engineering?

A: YES.At Ofin Global Engineering we design custom made Cold Rooms. We take time to understand our customer's unique requirement and custom our design to meet their specific and unique demand.

Q: On what power supply does the Ofin Global Engineering Cold Rooms operate on?

A: Our Cold Room machines are designed to operate on any 3-phase power source. Our electric motors operate on 415 volts, 50Hz, 3-phase AC power source.

The power source could be from the National power grid, or a standard 3-phase generator.

Also we now design energy conservative machines that can operate on solar energy power sources.

Q: Does Ofin Global Engineering provide maintenance on only Cold Rooms installed by you?

A: YES we do. At Ofin Global Engineering we understand the importance of periodic maintenance activities for machines, this is why one of our core services in the company is the Annual Maintenance Contract (AMC).

The AMC is a comprehensive maintenance package which our clients are encouraged to subscribe to in order to take up all the cold room maintenance responsibilities on our own. You can check our service section to learn more.

Q: Is there a discount on maintenance if the Cold Room was installed by Ofin Global Engineering?

A: YES! Once your cold room has been installed by us we take the cold room as our baby, and we give it the top routine and corrective maintenance care it requires for optimum and reliable performance at a discounted price.

Q: How much does a Cold Room by Ofin Global Engineering cost?

A: The cost of a Cold Room varies, it depends on the design and the capacity of the cold room in question. You can see the Cold Room price list for more details.

Q: How can I reach Ofin Global Engineering for a Cold Room?

A: Ofin Global HVAC&R Engineering has a physical office at:39, Olufemi street, Ikola Ilumo Lagos Agbado, Oke Odo 100001, Lagos State, Nigeria.

Contact us via:
Call:08063150242, 09022892870
Email: info@ofinglobal.com
Website: https://g.co/kgs/WepqYS.
Linkedin: https://www.linkedin.com/company/ofin-global-engineering.

CHAPTER 10: FAQ WITHOUT A WEBSITE.

Let it be known that businesses with presence on Facebook already have a platform for an FAQ section.

Facebook wants to help small businesses build structure like the big boys (Businesses) so they have made provisions for FAQ but only on pages not your personal timeline.

Here is a step by step guide on how to input your questions.

1. Make a list of questions.

2. Answer them using the steps in the previous chapters.

3. Go to your Facebook page.click on your business page.

4. In the below example:my personal account on Facebook is DNA Imprints Nmaele,my brand page is : Beyond Bullying.

5. Then follow the steps in this screenshots.I
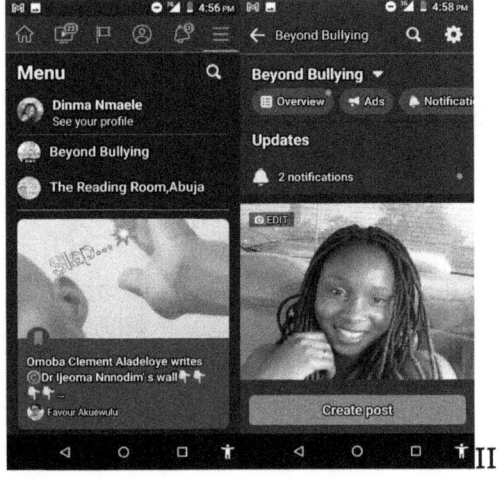
II

THE FAQ GUIDE

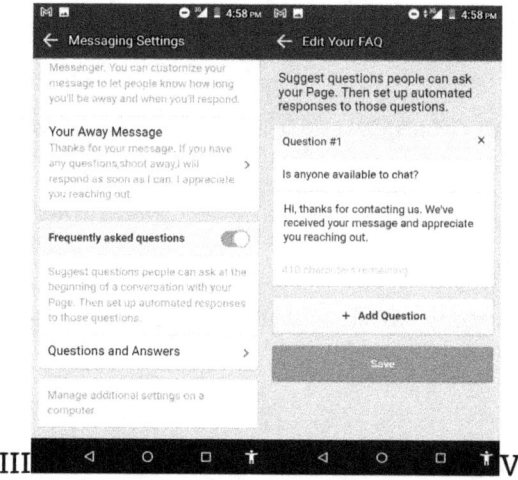

All of these steps would take you to your destination.

Congratulations! you now have an FAQ on your business Facebook page.

Bonus:

Above all, I want your business to succeed.

Here is a way to make it happen.

An efficient website is expensive to create & manage but we need one to launch our businesses on a large scale so I want to show you a way out.

Hear the good news,you can have your own website for free on 'Selar'.

You only pay a transaction fee when you make sales,not a minute before.

You can choose to let your customer pay the transaction fee.

I am coming to the best part:
- You don't pay maintenance fees.
- You can accept payment in 8 different currencies.
- You can sell digital products via Selar.
- You can use Selar for classes, sell products & so, tutorials,create affiliates etc.
- You can use the platform for services that require subscriptions from your customers.
- You get your money in less than 24 hours when paid in your local currency.
- For foreign currency,you get the most favorable exchange rate paid into your local bank account.
- Customers are required to fill in their data before purchase.
- You can export this data into your device giving you a credible contact list (email & phone numbers) of your customers.
- With a website on Selar,you look credible to prospective customers.

- You sell at any time, from anywhere to anyone.

Excited? Click here to join millions of others.

or visit www.selar.co

CONCLUSION

Congratulations!!!

If you are on this page, it means your FAQ is ready on your jot-pad next to you.

Having problems figuring out how to begin or you are stuck.

Close your eyes, take a deep breath and exhale.

Still not feeling better, take a fifty minute break, take a walk , anything that distracts you.

The words will sink a little deeper this time or try it out some other time.

Still don't understand or you simply don't want to write yourself.

Then send a message to get one dnaimprints@gmail.com

GLOSSARY

FAQ: FREQUENTLY ASKED QUESTIONS

LAQ: LEAST ASKED QUESTIONS

Q&A : QUESTIONS AND ANSWERS.

ABOUT THE AUTHOR

Dinma Nmaele-Afam

Dinma is a certified Linguist and Founder of DNA Imprints, a brand that specializes in writing Biographies, Memoirs, Publishing and Speech Reading in Africa.

Dinma has several publications to her name.

BOOKS BY THIS AUTHOR

A Childhood Snatched By School

September 2001, Dinma's parents made a decision that would change her life forever.

They sent her to a boarding school at age 8, there she would experience abuse, untold hardship and almost lose one eye.

This book talks about Dinma's experience as a child "Rushed through school" because of her intelligence, the loopholes in the Nigerian Educational system (boarding schools) and offers solutions to prevent it from happening to any other Nigerian child.

This is a must READ if you are a parent, teacher or education enthusiast, investor in the Nigeria system.

We can change the world, one child at a time!

www.ingramcontent.com/pod-product-compliance
Lightning Source LLC
Chambersburg PA
CBHW050305230526
45471CB00005B/2029